Elizabeth Seydel Morgan

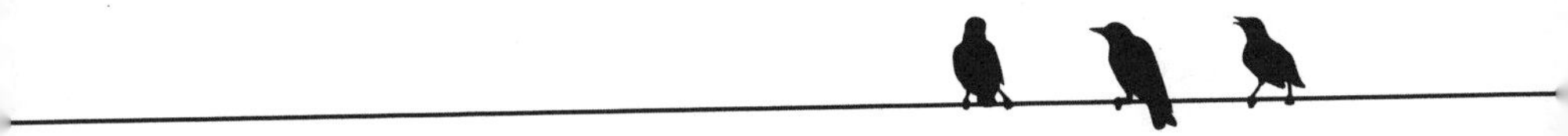

Without a Philosophy

poems

Louisiana State University Press ⚜ *Baton Rouge*

Published by Louisiana State University Press

Manufactured in the United States of America
First printing

Designer: Michelle A. Garrod
Typeface: Utopia
Printer and binder: Edwards Brothers, Inc.

Library of Congress Cataloging-in-Publication Data

Morgan, Elizabeth Seydel, 1939–
Without a philosophy : poems / Elizabeth Seydel Morgan.
p. cm.
ISBN-13: 978-0-8071-3229-6 (alk. paper)
ISBN-13: 978-0-8071-3230-2 (pbk. : alk. paper)
I. Title
PS3563.O828W58 2007
811'.54—dc22

2006038566

A number of the poems in this collection first appeared in the following journals: *Appalachian Life:* "Rescue Me"; *Blackbird:* "Caretaker," "Drawing Lesson: Outline and Edge," "The Melancholy Tailor"; *Five Points:* "The Birthday"; *New Virginia Review:* "The Californian"; *Poetry:* "Euripides' Cave"; *Quarterly West:* "Black Animals," "Transient"; *Shenandoah:* "Blessing the Watersnakes"; *64:* "Seven Ages of Man: Saturday, Virginia Division of Motor Vehicles"; *Solo:* "How Space Travel Affects the Aging"; *Southern Review:* "Without a Philosophy"; *Traffic Report:* "Make Yourself at Home."

The author is grateful for fellowships to the Virginia Center for the Creative Arts, where many of these poems were written.

The paper in this book meets the guidelines for permanence and durability of the Committee on Production Guidelines for Book Longevity of the Council on Library Resources. ♾

Winner of the L. E. Phillabaum Poetry Award for 2007

for Susan Cofer and Mimi Seydel
and
in memory of Don Cooke

Contents

Transient

The Impossibility of Gauging Distances

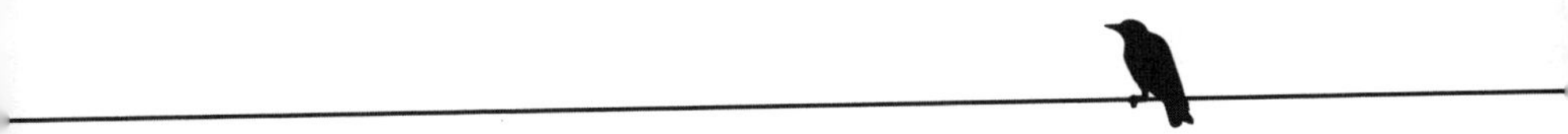

Without a Philosophy

. . . like a dog between 4 trees . . .
—e-mail from a friend

Toward the end of this summer,
this long labyrinth,
I thought of you in a clearing
green and sunlit, bordered by four
tall trees and the dusky spaces
between them where barely
discernible rhododendron
start the process of shadows.

Light moves on your turning
shoulders and on the four tall trees:
the black walnut, the copper beech,
two sycamores peeling to bonewhite
the sun loves most.

It's not only the trees but more
than your fabled dog's choices;
it's those darknesses between
that like me you are lured to choose.

But you are arrested there—
watching the swallowtails
feed on the aster, then go in
and disappear.

Diagnosis, after Dickinson

Increments of information
Slant upward from the shock
That forms the quadrilateral fact—
Base of solid rock

Increments of information
Slowly pyramid—
We're either learning more each day
Or slantedly misled

Increments of information
Are all that we can bear—
Giving hope of pinnacle
While pointing to the air

Bombing Yugoslavia

Blue Ridge Mountains, April 1999

Goldfinches squabble for the broken peg
perch at the thistle-seed feeder. Blood
red cardinals fight for territory
in the forsythia hedge—redder than ever
against that gold explosion
waving its tendrils in uncertain sun.
For now the winds are massing clouds,
gray rollers on the ridges to the east.

The groundhog's up and out and down,
undermining everything.
I can push a rock against his hole
but it's hopeless, he'll get around it
like the poison ivy's early shoots
that won't be stopped by any herbicide
I spray, no nipping this one in the bud, its invasion
is accomplished by July.
Meadow grass has sprung above surprises
and you have to walk with care across it now.
Ground bees are up. The snake's awake.
The snake, in fact, I saw today and shuddered;
its head was in the bluebirds' house.
Its long tail dangled out the augured hole.

Out here planting lilies at the border,
I'm struck by blood
along the blue vein of my wrist.
A jagged rock? A barb of buried wire?
It's blood I've come here to forget, fought
the thoughts all day: your open chest in Boston,
the roadsides out of Kosovo.

The Well

They stride in garish clothes—dayglow
orange, purple fleece, tweeds—nothing
matches. Their voices babble and clash
in cacophony nobody hushes.

Most drive their bodies like madmen,
perpetrating purpose, cells
to their ears, striding the streets
straight ahead.

Though there are some who saunter
with no protocol,
with the brainless insouciance
of all the time in the world.

There is no reason
for their delusion, their lack of decorum.
Unfazed by fact, they go about
their suspicious business.

Struck by sun, not one
of the well ever looks up
here to the hospital window,
even shading his eyes with his hand.

Unanswered Questions

Like these: what is this expression
on the face of the woman
in the foreground of the photograph
of the Hartford circus fire of 1944?
Why, to my eyes, does she seem calm,
detached from the calamity, ignoring the conflagration
of tentless timbers, the black billows behind her?
Can't she smell? Doesn't she hear the screams?
But my eyes are wrong enough these days to keep
a magnifying glass on my bedside table
and at the end of another day of knowing nothing
of what it is like to be you, of how you can bear
your burning fate, I bring the glass down
on the photograph to the people escaping the fire,
pass the man closest to the camera whose mouth
forms the classic *O* of tragedy,
round down on the placid woman
behind him in her unruffled summer dress
and I'm frightened by her magnified face
that is nothing but pixels of an image,
some dots clustered, some spaced.

Drawing Lesson: Outline and Edge

An outline surrounds a form that is no longer there.
—Eleanor Rufty

Like this drawing by my mother of my baby hand,
the plump, splayed fingers outlined in waxy crayon.

Or the body on the sidewalk:
here's where it was when it fell.
Flat blue chalk shows he raised his hands.

Where is the form no longer there?
If auras of angels were outlines
who knows where the angel flew?
Or the victim, bagged and borne away.
Or myself, in nineteen forty-two.

The line dies, says the artist,
if it only outlines. Think of a line as an edge,
as the edge of a form
that is moving away from you in space.

And I do, as I trace your profile,
your edges, the slope of your shoulders
while you sit by the fire, curved to the book
you hold with both hands.

Watering

I have watered and watered hundreds of feet
of a cracked clay field where we put in new grass,
as the dry summer day took its slow time to end.

Now I pace in the dark I came back to let happen,
the water turned off at the spigot like hope,
like the dumb trust I could conquer a killing drought,
wet down half a baked acre with a nozzleless hose.

After your call I watered the bed where we slept
and watered the kitchen where we danced late at night
and watered this farmhouse I love and have wondered
if I'd love it without love always hovering.

But the air cracks and crazes in the hot silent rooms
like the packed earth stifling its own life
and tears are as futile as a garden hose
when the skies hold back rain without mercy.

Shutters

Through the slanted louvers, light
cracks the shadowed room; October
Sunday afternoon asserts its life.
Slats of brightness on your blanket
insist the sky outside is cold blue.

Your cheeks would redden like leaves
if only you could rise and come outside.
We could breathe bracing, electric air.
We could walk,
walk fast to keep warm
because there's a chill out there in the park
though the grass is still green
and most of the trees here in Louisville
haven't faced the fact of frost. I can't sit still,
leafing *The Times* as you lie there.
Its pages litter the light-barred floor.

But who am I to feel so stuck inside,
for we both know the truth
that when we were young I spent
so many golden Sunday afternoons
in shuttered rooms. Crack a cold beer
and oh how we loved shutting out the sun,
some football game droning
its thudding plays beneath our breathing.

Walking across the Border

Why would a man
hardly standing
want to walk
to Tijuana?

To be hit in the face with heat,
with dirt and tawdry,
with clusters of dissolute men
and the hover of poverty?

But above all, why
would a man
hardly standing
want to walk
to Tijuana
on the arm of his spoiled woman
whose eyes could only see
the dirt and tawdry,
the hover of poverty.

He would have it no other way
but to walk into Tijuana
across the curdled river
and its concrete banks.

He was sick as the dogs on the sidewalk,
weak as the short old women peddling beads;
he knew his number was up.
But he'd insisted it would be a lark
to push our bodies against the man-sized turnstile
and walk
from California into Mexico.

I've memorized his pale face
as he held on to me through a throng of men

vying for dollars on the main street of Tijuana.
He said with his unfailing candor, I hate
that I couldn't protect you . . .

From what, said the spoiled woman, unafraid and dumb.
He didn't answer as he pushed us on
but his eyes matched the eyes of the Mexicans
pressing around us—men fighting for life.

The Glutton of Grief

Over the funeral meats
the glutton of grief
holds the oily chop
to the teeth, gobbles
the plump loin,
slurps the goblet
the left hand holds,
dribbles at the lips,
the eyes. Unseemly
gurgles, moans, no one
else at the table
could be so hungry, no
one else is even there
at the laden board.

Then they *are* there,
holding their polite plates.

Sweep it all into your mouth.
Let them starve.

The Present

I guess it's not unexpected
that it's taken longer to stop
indulging the colorful flashbacks
—just like a movie
—almost as corny, with music
—with the trick of the blur, the swirl,

so driving past "Naughties" on Broad Street
I see him so clearly, I let the whole scene unspool:
he leaves here for some reason,
he leaves here for some reason, and returns.

His is the energy of happiness,
his smile and the sly/shy offering
of the penis-tipped lipstick—
it's his present for the day.
How could someone so present be so dead.

December 2001

In the hundred hues of sorrow
Tonight is the color of fog
No memory of your face
How could that be?
All day I've been sick to my stomach
I suspect the mail, so empty
Of you, so full of spores
I make another drink anyway

Were you once right here?
Why can't I picture you doing
That little tap-step by the stove.

Driving Alone

Months of miles down the mourning road
here's the stab of *left out.* The cut
in the heart that must first have been made
when eight girls in sixth grade
turned their backs on me
at a round table for eight.

Fifty years later I'm driving past
a circle of men in front of Dodd's Store
and I ache to know what they're saying—
the same with the couple in a truck I'm behind
who're taking the curves down the mountain
slow, leaning toward one another—
and later, the clutch of women in a church
parking lot who know some secret
that's making them laugh.
Then I get hurt by the birds on a wire,
their heads all bent in the same direction,
hurt that I don't know what kind they are
or where they are going or what they eat—
and I'm stung by my failure to identify
a single tree that I pass in its pale new leaf
except a dogwood in its wounded white.
And I actually start crying when I see ahead
a perfectly tilled red rectangle of garden
because I don't know how it was plowed
or who worked it. Or where he is now.

Restart

I have begun to admire things that work
(the hands-up wine opener
pops the cork)
and things that restart—
the car when you start it, such a simple twist of the wrist,
the furnace,
after being locked in the basement
with nothing to do for five months,
clicks, harrumphs, bangs, blows.
Flick on the hair dryer, the clothes dryer,
the houselights: they volt to life and warmth.

Here in the U.S.A., you come to count
on things that restart.
We expect ignition;
we trust in liftoff.
Even the old lawnmower, with enough muscle,
will sputter under its choke, then fill its bag with air.

Today the car is covered with snow, a motionless mound
on the driveway. Inside it's an ice cave, lit with pale light.
Silent and blind, it's a strange inhabited copy of its self.

The igloo light is enough to see by.
The key to the ignition switch, the practiced turn,
the press of the foot,
the engine clears its throat.
It blows its own cold breath.
Why couldn't you?

Imaginary Therapy

You're told there's been a war
and you were in it:
a lethal beach

a flooded trench—or the war
that bloodied your young mind,
the one in a jungle of green and straw, hot
sun, hot rain, explosions at every step
of a maze without ins or ends
where you were dropped.

So you bend low and trudge your jungle
heavy and hot behind your bayonette
and your friends ahead start dying.
And die, and die and then it's your friend
beside you and you hold his head up
against your breast and search
any sky you can see for a chopper.

After starting with war, you admit you're a woman.
You know about choppers from movies.
The men you know who went don't talk.

The imaginary therapist considers you.

The return is wordless, he says.
How can you speak in a country
with no words for horror?

Or write, you think, from its corridor.

The Impossibility of Gauging Distances

If she could gauge the distance between the blurred dark figure
at the edge of the photograph of a winter beach—northern
    Spain—
and herself, so foregrounded her bad tooth shows,
she could start understanding them

If she could gauge the distance between a cluttered desk in
    the mountains
of Virginia and a garage stacked with books in a working-class
neighborhood in snowbound Boston
she could start understanding

What is the measure between sides of a bed, the seconds it takes
love to fly between Riga and Richmond—if only
she'd studied the laws of time and measurement
she could start

What is the distance between the sixties of the last century
and the ashes falling on New York? If she could gauge the
    distance
between a figure on a beach in San Sebastian and where he
    went in 2001,
she could

Clean-Up

How long can I keep cleaning
out drawers
before the ground of words
begins to crack open
and all the ordered drawers
splinter against the flung walls,
the plastic computer shatters
into shards of gray and its chips
full of old words unwind their tiny wires
into the updraft?
So what, these minutes of order will honor the past.
And show what I'm able to throw away
which is just about everything.
But not everything.
In the silence before the sirens, the aftershocks,
I believe your Post-it note and the Westin pen
will find their way back from the scattered trash
and join the new words
that will stick to scraps of anything
stacking haphazardly,
waiting for drawers to box them in.

Watching the Weather Channel

Watching the Weather Channel

Is it raining on you, Linda,
down in San Antonio—
raining too much?
Here in Virginia
the grass breaks
under our feet; the creek's
left stones for cows to lick.
The TV screen shows us cracks
in the earth where there used to be hay,
simulated systems massing
and fading over the globe.
We say we pray for rain
but what do we know
about asking for what we need?
We pray for the hurricane
to go around *you*—but send us its fringe,
the way we pray for the hand of Death
to pass on to another geography.

E-mail to Odessa

Love watches the weather of where you are,
Checks every channel and paper to know
When your skies are cloudy or full of snow,
When your moonless night holds no bright star.

If love's hot sun can reach so far
Love wants to melt your wintry blow,
Wrap its warm breezes around you, so
Love watches the weather of where you are.

The Dry Years

T. S. Eliot must have been outside—
though it's hard to picture him in his vest and tie,
sitting on a porch in a rocking chair as I am now—
waiting for rain. I thought of him when I heard the crickets,
cicadas, I'd say, the only sound in this strange dry dusk.
It's 9 p.m., late in the summer of 2002, still the light
behind the mountain, still the suggestion of a sun
that's been hidden all day behind clouds
which shifted, and darkened once, and tonight even gave
off a rumble like thunder. More than one . . .
The grass is so dry it crackles under your soles, it
sticks like splinters if you walk barefoot to the hose
that comes from the spring box that comes from the spring,
hose barely trickling this afternoon when I placed it
under the American chestnut sapling.

I decide what to water these past three years
by how long it will last if it makes it.
The American chestnut is an experiment.

It's almost dark now and I haven't heard a usual sound,
no mountain stream, no danger huffs of does or noises
in the woods that sound like cries, not even the wild beagles
that can yelp through the night if they're onto something.
Not the rustle of poplar leaves, or the giant sycamore
or the call of a single mourning dove. Just this rasp: crickets,
or cicadas. And a couple of claps of thunder.
How did that young poet in England know
about drought? The kind that comes from lack of water?
There must have been a time he sat outside listening,
maybe in Missouri, waiting for rain.

Cow Bone Clearing

From down in the hollow all afternoon
cows moan and bellow. How
could I know. On Long Mountain
I've heard their voices, the lowing,
the call and response of one cow
to another, a calf to a mother,
a mother to calf. But still from below
into the gold of the walnut's falling,
evening of first month of fall, still
the chorus of bellowing rises
like earth turning dark behind me
and now
in an hour before dawn I sit at the window
and look down the unceasing
sound in the dark and I know
the ache of a mother.
The loss like no other.
We allow even cows our pity for hours,
for the gorging milk, the unsuckled bloat,
the absence below,
in a meadow of shadows.

Not long ago I followed
a trail off the old Bough Road
down through thick laurel and cedar
and discovered a clearing where
flickers of sunlight fell on white bones—
cow skulls staring, a score of white skulls,
a row of curved ribs,
pearled pelvic rounds—
and though not a bird or a cricket called
it seemed that the sound I hear now from the hollow
rose from that bone ground, long and low.

Everybody's Coming in for the Winter

The slick furred mouse scratches and scumbles
somewhere between the walls of my bedroom
and the sheathing of this old house. Between
the ceiling and shingles a squirrel gallops.
Damn them, noises in the dark, invisible squatters
it's taken me years to identify—
it's the groundhog under the flooring
who bumps and grinds to deepen his burrow.
But why so early, gnawing around in my inner mazes,
when summer's long season has not let go?
I'm listening, sleepless alone in our bed,
to the sounds of aliveness moving in:
How do they know
in the summery southern middle of night
that it's time to leave the kudzu caves,
the grassy banks, the fields and trees?
How do the creatures clambering around me
know it's time, know it's time, know it's time
to come in.

Late Winter, Starling and Apricot

Under the dull hill, the lowering sky,
the flowering apricot lives
up to its name, its brown sticks dotted
with blossoms—of all incongruous colors
here on a mountain in winter: pink.
Inside the cold cabin
in the sooty cave of the wood stove
a black bird lumps like char.
I pick it out to the light
with a piece of newsprint
I'd plan to kindle and see
it's a starling, barely dead. Not black.
Its feathers are iridescent, dotted all over
with bright white spots. Its glassy eye
is colorless. You could say black,
but out at the foot of the flowering tree
it reflects a gray sky
full of apricots.

Log

The axed oak tops
the drying stack, grows hollow
and no more knows
its emptiness
than the bird that grips
and pecks its grubby bark.

The log sustains him,
provides as well as any sap-thick
branch—and better—
it isn't troubled by the winds.

But touch this log to kindled coals
and, hungrier than birds,
fire finds out—
flames to the inmost edge of surface,
defines the core of nothing
in burning circumference.

Suddenly the City Swept the Street

March fifteenth, cold as a warning:
Beware!

Last fall's oak leaves, raked
as separate leather gloves, muck

in black piles at the curb, the promise
of pickup broken by snows,

delay, a dozen sleets and freezing rains,
motor oil, mud, flood and flu—

So I screamed at the Ides out my window:
Taxes, taxes, take up my leaves!

Some love take my crabby heart!
Some force unsuck the tentacles of winter!

When suddenly—this afternoon—
the city swept the street.

Clean street, now meet Equinox:
Who knows what may happen next.

Stingy

It's life with your sourapple aunt
whose mouth
is pursed like pulled drawstrings
into
an inverted *u*—
this stingy Spring.

What could blossom
in the face of her disdain?
Who could open to her flint-thin arms?

The pear trees on the mountainside shiver
in her sheer winds, seal shut their buds
that are glazed with cold rain. Today
beige grass is speckled with frost,
the wheelbarrow's full of frozen water.

This time last year, the pear trees had bloomed;
by now they had petaled the meadow and drifted
white dots on the breeze to the greening grass.
Newborn calves lay in the sun by their mothers.

Today is one more withholding.
Nothing's
let loose to live its life.
A shrinking spirit
skulks on the ridges,
bulked only by coats
like the dull grey feathers of finches
who wait for warmth to turn gold
as they peck at the seedblown thistles.
We wait
for warmth too,
like tight buds, the roots
of peonies, the snake under the cold holding tank.

We wait for warmth to uncurl us, to disrobe us,
to pull us up and out.

We await generosity,
grateful that it's only late.

Flasher

Look! This is the last time
we'll see the giant sycamore
flashing the mountain,
stripped to the muscular trunk
it would take the whole family
to embrace.

Its white arms still shock us.
It dropped everything in the fall—
every facade, every screen, the leaves
and covers of every neighbor
(except the dotted evergreens)
even peeling what we would call skin.

In winter its bones drove the negative:
white branches, white branches,
against not much else but leafmold beige
and charcoal gray. Who would
have thought—until it bared all—
it was wider than the mountainside,
that it reached up past the ridge?

Just this week the minor maples, poplars,
old service trees, new dogwood,
who knows what all, fuzzed up with buds
and from this point on, the X-ray blurs.
Soon the sycamore's glowing bones
will disappear in a crowd of green
like Daphne's fingers turning into laurel,
leaving Apollo confused in leaves.

Redbud, Dogwood and Crow

Jesus! If I saw a tree deep pink as dawn,
another white as a weightless cloud, I'd doubt
the first was called a Judas tree, the other's
blossoms meant to depict the nailholes of Christ.
I would say nothing so cheerful, so vitally Spring,
could speak of betrayal, or bloom as suffering.
I'd call in that crow over there
to flap over to the redbud, then
fly up to a high dogwood branch,
and sit.
A big patch of black
crowing like a rowdy drunk
siphoning misnomers from innocence
and shouting them into the wind.

Transient

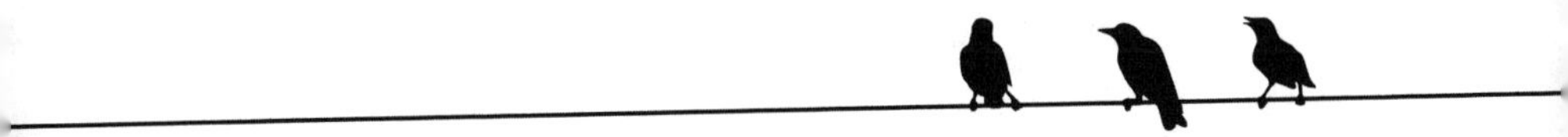

Transient

for Craig Pleasants

Widening circles of thin gold swamp grass,
the tip of each blade held by the hollow stem of another,
float down from the ceiling.

The eye sees one airy spiral of grasses—
not the invisible filaments the circles are held by—
a spiral that hovers, trembled by breeze.

Craig named it Transient and hung it in a show.
But afterward, even collapsed on the roof of his van,
it flew away when his back was turned.

A true transient, I said, but he didn't smile.
He found it later, broken, in a ditch,
and set to work at once on restoration.

Craig knows that art is figurative language,
that the person sleeping against the tile
in the Greyhound restroom is real.

That our hovering stay is short.
But the made thing is beauty all itself;
it is here, now, trembling from the ceiling.

What is fleeting, what is flown
is its conception. The idea
the creator knows, and lets go.

The Melancholy Tailor

It seemed everything he stitched was a destiny.
As he pinned up the shoulders, the darts
under the breasts, the hems of the trousers
he felt as close to their futures
as he was to their bodies.

When he fitted the pleatless pants of the groomsman
he knew a bridesmaid would unzip them.
Oh he hemmed her waltz-length taffeta too.
And her sister's. And the moonfaced roommate's
from New York. He knew which of the aqua
dresses would flow down like a wave
to the feet of the kissing couple. He made little tucks
to flatter the roommate's waistline.

Velcro he scoffed at way past its invention.
But the fingerless kid from the war in Vietnam
came in and said "Velcro." With his paws he pointed
to zipper and buttons. "Next week," said the tailor,
planning his order. He saw the man fastening
his own coats and pants, ripping off his own clothes
with the drama of sound, doing whatever
in the rest of his life he chose to do.

The CEO was sizing down. This man's waist
went in, and in again. Was it sex or sickness?
The tailor tried not to wonder, though he knew
either way, it wouldn't work out. He fitted
such clients with weight-loss in silence,
kneeling before them to taper the legs,
his mouth full of pins.

Once, when he was thirty, he had measured
from the cowlneck, long-sleeved top
to the slit, tight skirt's hem, a dress of pale velvet.

She stood on his new-painted platform
turning when he said turn
as he pinned in every inch to fit
her elongated, sinuous curves.

And after she was gone, he held the gown
against him with one arm and with the other
swept his sewing table clean of clothes.
He stitched and stitched at the small black machine.
And the juddering noise, his deft foot on the treadle,
the flow of warm velvet through his fingers
was the last time he didn't know what would happen.

You, Archie Ammons

A. R. Ammons (1926–2001)

You're now a *curl of motion spent,*
edited into the anthologies, misunderstood
in the valleys and lichen-ledges

But much that you said
I took in, how to catch Spring
a second go-round by climbing

a mountain, how to write short
and live long, how to bray
shy as a trillium

and find eternity in a grain
of garbage, so much you
thought, you taught me to think

along with you, the improbability
of a caring cosmos, the notion of whether
we're cared for or not, we're in it for keeps.

How Space Travel Affects the Aging

1. What Their Bodies Know

They're not used to it.
There's a lot their bodies have learned
to endure,
though,
facing a mirror or fingers—
yours or someone else's—
where a part of you is missing
or added.
Gravity
too little, too much
floating, free-falling, pinned to the Earth
in magnetic boots going nowhere.
Thus patience in one place—
a sightseer unable to hike mysterious
mountains seen from a window,
take the old bike up those blue curves
or swim for miles in a foreign sea.
Sight: eyes will not be portholes long.
Perspective:
how space travel affects the aging
is a question that makes them laugh.
They know where they're going next.

2. Italics Mine

> Researchers hope the sleep experiment will help explain why so many astronauts sleep one to three hours less each night in orbit than they do on Earth, and *why the elderly tend to have trouble sleeping on Earth.*
>
> —The Associated Press

trouble sleeping on Earth
trouble sleeping on Earth
troubled sleepers on Earth
Earth on sleeping trouble

one hundred, ninetyfive
ninety, eightyfive, eight-
-y, seventyfive, seventy.
sixtyfive, sixty, fiftyfive
trouble sleeping on Earth
Earth. Earth. Earth. Earth

earth hearth heart further
heart hurt hear ear earth
birth breathe eat beat be
trouble sleeping on
earth trouble sleeping
on earth trouble
sleeping on earth

3. John Glenn Hires Literary Agent

The Associated Press, November 3, 1998

But when he came down
he found he was wordless
having stored so few in his life

when it came down to
writing about it he found
he kept thinking of birds

how when they come down
from the air they're at home in
they perch on a branch and sing

4. How the Aging Affect Space Travel

No crew
No tests
Below
Just Blue
And you,
Weightless

Singapore Art Museum in the Rain

More than a century of sticky boys
and Christian Brothers sweating in long robes
raised their faces to the open arches
when a hot wind blew down the Straits
rattling the palm fronds that clicked
like marbles in a bag, or bamboo sticks played
down louvered shutters by students out
to make a clatter.

Now the boys and brothers gone,
the old verandas have been glazed
with ultraviolet-blocking windows
that in this gallery protect the replica
of Leonardo's flying man.

A guard barks twice, a black-eyed child
from Thailand withdraws his starfish hand
from an invention of the man of Vinci
who couldn't keep his hands off anything.

Suddenly outside the graygreen glass
the famous rain of Singapore
spills down the afternoon,
pours through glistening frets of palm leaves,
glazes the black taxies on Bras Basah Road.
And where the gutters meet the corners,
water arcs like fountains.

Inside, the priceless Leonardo painting
flown over the Red and Arabian Seas,
the tip of India, the Bay of Bengal:
John the Baptist as a Youth,
a curlyhaired Italian with a secret smile,
a boy who could be gazing out the window
contemplating water.

Make Yourself at Home

Fingering their unfamiliar keys,
over their good tea I read the map
she sketched on a napkin.
It's not far to the museum
and I've got hours before my train.

On their third floor I walk naked
to the skylighted shower and
wash my hair in apricot shampoo, steam
bright air with clouds of sudsy fruit,
then turbaned in a thick white towel,
wrap myself in the man-sized guest robe.

I set out to investigate, to pry
this happy pair from what I heard at dinner,
to learn a life I hardly know
and so I go
down to his study.

It seems to me his books on politics,
antiquities and legal legends spell virility
like the soft cracked leather chair, the smell
of pipesmoke, tortoise framed soft-focused
nine by twelve of her in black and white on his
emaculate and polished walnut table.
Early in the morning I've made her man my hero.

While her own one's-own-room is too
a place to crave, books ordered but askew, plants
greening at the tall and narrow sunbright window,
postcards propped, exotic or amusing, in shelves
and cubbies (surely meant for me to read),
everything Eudora Welty ever wrote
—plus her picture—above
the row of photos of my hostess and her husband.

In one I lift and hold, he looks at her and smiles
as she bends to autograph her latest book.
On the teakwood desk, a dozen maps,
a sheaf of papers by the laptop.

I dare their bedroom for more clues. The unlocked
door is closed, but swings into a room from a motel:
featureless and tidied. The king-sized bed is made.
Had I hoped for tortured sheets, dregs of wine in
glasses on the floor?
Do they make this bed together, pull from either side,
neatly tucking his and hers before they leave for work?

I itch with an urge to rummage,
to ransack his desk for the note so wracked
its longing has to be illicit,
discover the cache of unspeakable photos he took
through a crack of her and another,
root through her closet, uncover
the smudged and rough-thumbed
cards stuffed in a video box,
the cellular phone wrapped in a scarf.
I search through her cabinet for
the little brown vial of white powder,
crawl under their bed to find in the dark
a mess of tangled leather ropes.

Nothing. But sudden shame at the naked legs
that are mine sticking out
through the tassels of the spread.

Dressed and coated, I check the latch,
leave with the keys to their home.
As they directed, I'm off to visit
their classical museum
where polished objects on display
will claim to tell a human story.

Seven Ages of Man: Saturday, Virginia Division of Motor Vehicles

First, the smooth-cheeked boy
whose mother holds the papers.
She wants to know if he can get his learner's
permit without a birth certificate.
He's wordless, looks as if he'll die
if he's refused. She looks as if she doesn't
know that from this moment he is gone.

Next, the kid in hip-hop pants and pierced-ear
silver hunches over Regulations of the Road.
Concentration outweighs cool. His right leg dances.
It could be the only test he's taken yet
with every brain cell surging.

Young man with the incongruous grin,
sleepy-eyed, disheveled, explains his stolen
wallet, what a mystery last night, what
in the world can he do now, he has to be
in Charlottesville this afternoon.

Then the couple hung with diaper bags
and babies. One toddler on her hip, another
aiming for the brown-skinned boy his own age
across the room. The husband with an infant
in a Snugli on his chest retrieves his kid, sullenly
ignores the baby-loving smiles of all the crowd
who're not with babies.

A well-dressed woman clicks across the marble
(imitation marble over concrete) floor. She's suited
for a luncheon somewhere else, holds her license tag
where everyone can see its seven letters (the limit
in Virginia): JAGUAR 9.

The immigrant, flamboyant coal black hair
a wreath around her pale, uncomprehending
face is told she needs not just her passport but
some proof of residence in Richmond. She takes
this fact with calm beyond our local powers.

And then there's me, number C-nine-five,
a girl who was here in 1960,
barely believing I'm here once again, nervous again
at the DMV, sixty and scared of the vision test
as that kid who goes over and over the rules.
I'm practicing looking.
And willing to wait, like everyone here,
for the license to drive.

The Person behind Me Is Talking in Numbers

The person behind me is talking in numbers—
and like Robert Penn Warren on that night
flight when he was considering Emerson
who'd left out evil in the bottom layer
of his two-ply map of America,
I'm looking down the night sky
at the darkening earth and listening.
This is a mystery.
This woman's voice is as unmodulated
as engine drone: *five seven one three two*
one eight five six four three four nine one
and I'm suddenly wondering if maybe
my only language is one that nobody knows,
that she is speaking the lingua franca
and I am alone with my language of pictures.

(I didn't remember but now I revise this to bow
to Warren who wrote in the very poem
I partly recalled—
"Homage to Emerson on Night Flight to New York"—
that the man next to him was reciting,
out of fear, like a prayer, the multiplication table.
So. Was it this buried fact
that connected his night flight to mine?
I'd like to think the connection was thinking
about thinking and how rooted fathers could
get it wrong. But it's about language,
again, isn't it ?)

What would Warren have done
with the view of our blue world from space?
He would have seen the full color print—
but by then his perspective was graphed
like the ruled lines in etchings
and like Emerson walking across Boston Common,
his peripheral vision left some things out.

Now only the little lights are on in the plane
that drones me home to Virginia, the clustered
little lights below, and the lady behind me
who speaks in one-digit numbers
intones all nine as a lullaby.

My forehead is cold on the porthole;
behind it I'm thinking of Warren who longed
for the darkness to fill up with stars
like the lights of the Earth he flew home to,
loving even its evil, even its babel.

The Californian

Larry Levis, in memory

It was almost fall in the Blue Ridge
and among these small mountains
he seemed content to be so far east.

He leaned against the doorjamb
blending his cigarette smoke with afternoon haze
and asked after the apples
dense on my tall, unpruned tree.

An old vineyard hand,
he knew the uses of the earth's fruits.

They go unpicked, I said.
The deer get the lower ones,
the groundhogs the windfall.
September, the air smells like brandy.

You need a ladder, he said.

This other August, the thunder over,
the lightning and downpour over,
as I walk out to the rain-soaked tree,
a heavily laden branch near the top
cracks and softly thrashes down.

In the gust of the after-breeze
the wet apple leaves sprinkle my hair
as I bend to pick from the broken bough—
for there on the earth
are the perfect ripe apples, glistening and easy,
easier than anyone has a right to expect.

Black Animals

If it had been a dream
interpreters would've had a field day.

For out of the field, that day,
a black bull appeared in my fenced yard,
and halfway through my cabin's opened door
a black snake nosed the air.

And I was obligated to be
down in the valley by sunset
to honor my friend from England.
I was already late and had to leave
a snake that was either inside or out
(he'd disappeared when I turned for something to throw)
and a black bull who might later be parked on
the unlit path to my door.

Is this enough information?
Will you ask what happened next?
Or can you imagine the drive in the dark after dinner
back up the mountain
only knowing what was ahead
by each higher curve
as it came in my headlights.
Can you realize this is the end of my story, and yours?

The Last Paintings of Manet

> Yesterday, Manet the painter suffered the amputation of a leg. Gangrene had set in and reduced the flesh to such a degree that the toenails came away upon contact.
> —*Le Figaro*, April 20, 1883

His last sixteen pictures are all
of flowers, small oils
of a few fresh stems
brought by friends to his bedside.

Most are in water, in one
of four glass vases
in his last room
or in his memory.

In the last painting of white lilacs,
in the flat-sided crystal vase,
the background is black.

The water and glass sparkle with white paint;
the edges of the lilac cones, massed and drooping
are flecks of white paint. The white dazzles flatly
against the deep black ground.

It is no sunny day by a trellis in Givergny.
City man, city man, they say
he loved Monet, but not nature.
Flowers were on bars in the Folies Bergere.
Nature was not on the mind of the man at the picnic.

In the last paintings of Manet
the quick stems in water delight us—
Lilacs, lilacs, green leaves and crystal—
though the light at the end of his brush is all there is.

Euripides' Cave

In Pericles' city, cold marble nights,
Protagoras, Socrates, pacing beside me,
ideas like stars arcing, or steadily blazing, or falling.
Mornings of papyri, mounting in rolls.
Reports of the War.

Afternoons, the agora, democracy's
broil. Men tricked out in the old dried skins
of politics, masculine voices
braying the many tongues of money,
reports from the War.
Believers bellowing gods like crowds at the races
urging their runner on with more noise.
So many signs to interpret—and I
with an eye for significance:
which citizen is rich, whose ignorance will kill
whose wife if back at home, unclasping
another man's warm gold necklace.

And all through the days of the sun,
the glare of the theater rising around me.
Tiers of men hoarding their careful prizes,
bearing down on my actors,
surrounding my circle of chosen words
with ceaseless mutter and drone.

There's a simple boat I can row
to Salamis.
In a cave I call mine
I fire my light.
In Salamis I wait for the women in silence.

Late sun falls on the stones of the entry
on the one sail in the dark blue Gulf.
It is so quiet, I hear Andromache crying,
Phaedra's whispers, Medea breathing
before the screams.

Prejudice

Stuck in a post-drink staring stint
I can't keep my eyes off the indigo bunting
bobbing his brilliance for seed after seed at my feeder.

But here's the catch: he's not brilliant this evening.
It's cloudy, almost dark, so is he—
it's just that I know from experience, as we say,
that he's blue.

He's almost a silhouette, uninteresting outline
not worth looking up, looking at.

But I keep watching, approving his appetite, wanting
this class of bird, these kinds of colors, here
in my neighborhood.

Stay here, I'm thinking, stay here, don't migrate somewhere.
Be blue for me. I'll never take my eyes off you. Even
at evening when you could be any dull bird
eating seed, nameless and plain.

The Birthday

I'm driving tonight into November.
The cold black sky is coming at me
and before I know it
it snuffs out the gold October glow
I left behind in Charlottesville,
those calendar leaves, the big ball sun
setting behind the rolling steeplechase—
its little obstacles casting shadows—
the lighted windows on the darkening hill,
silhouettes of hosts in my rearview mirror,
the last orange light on Foxfield Road.
Into the dark I can speed east and think
of the last night in October, Halloween,
when you were born thirty years ago.

Or I could not think of that night,
I know you'll be glad if I don't. It's still
today in Los Angeles, you're looking
for work. We're both looking for work
to keep us in days to get up.
I like this night highway blacking out
Autumn, making us one with all seasons.
Only my headlights and pairs of red taillights
ahead, you turning thirty where the leaves never
fall, the children not masked yet, the last sun
of the month still in the sky.

Tamed

What you were when they corralled you
I'm one of the few who know.

I was there, insouciant myself, leg hooked
over the railing, laughing with the hands.

Marveling. Black rebellion down from
the place we rode but couldn't stay.

Every single one of us
chewing on the long stems

hoped you'd bolt.

Oh, don't ride prettily. Don't.

Trampoline

Through the frame of a window on a northbound train
Stopped in the middle of the Illinois prairie
Where the fresh-turned earth is dark and wet and
Stretches black miles to a horizontal sky—
I'm looking at a child on a trampoline.

Oh what is she jumping for, jumping to see, jumping
For taller-than, jumping to be, jumping
To gaze at me on the train, jumping to rise
Again and again above that flat horizon?

That must be her mother who stands in the door
Wearing some kind of blue shirt and blue jeans,
Holding what looks like a magazine.
She seems to be calling or maybe she's screaming
At the child who is bouncing so close to a train.

Oh what is she jumping for, jumping to see, jumping
For taller-than, jumping to be, jumping
To gaze at me on the train, jumping to rise
Again and again above that flat horizon?

In school, her primary paintings of home
Must always be colored in parallel bands:
Railroad track, farmyard, wheatfield, sky.
The fields painted burnt-brown or golden or green
Depending on when in the school year she sees them.

Oh what is she jumping for, jumping to see, jumping
For taller-than, jumping to be, jumping
To gaze at me on the train, jumping to rise
Again and again above that horizon behind her?

On Reading Szymborska's "Starvation Camp near Jaslo"

It would be comforting to know
that being starved against your will
is like freezing to death.
Or like the way freezing to death has always
been described by the saved:
the mind curling the body into a kind of
tropical drowsiness.
"So warm, here . . ." a survivor said
of his wife's last words in the ice cave,
of her last improbably intimate smile.

Starving's hard,
we all know the first part—hunger.
Hunger the metaphor we also know:
standing in the kitchen,
staring into the bright, cold shelves
holding the door open
as if it too were a metaphor,
desiring nothing there, only
wanting to eat immortality or miracle
or change
or physical love.

But how hungry have you or I ever been?
At Jaslo "They were not given food, / all died."
The language is so basic it must translate
from Polish into anybody's words.

I wish I could know that past hunger,
into the icy cave of starve
the hallucination comes down around you
like a hot afternoon in Singapore
when sudden rain fills every pore with moisture,
your thousand mouths fill up with liquid,

up with food, for there in Jaslo
ripe fruits drop, and drop, softly and not too fast,
into your hands, calmly cupped.
You raise the tender pear to your lips, and eat.

Rescue Me

for Wayne and Robert

Metaphor fails
when you think about it.
Even though it's the underpinning of all
our understanding—
even the word understand
when you think about it
is a metaphor, there you are
standing under the fact of the rain
making it mean something
like—like?
Something like grief.

Watch the baby learn what like is,
quick as a wink.
Oh those little ones will wow you
understanding hiding,
understanding faces behind hands
are like disappearance—
but only like it—
and not gone forever.
A baby will always laugh
when the beloved face is rescued
by the parting of your hands.

Once I was rescued
not by a metaphor, not
by an agent of god,
not by a dove or an angel
but by two guys in a pickup truck
who drove up a hairpin road
to rescue a woman trapped
without food, without wood
near the top of a mountain.

They drove her down the curves of ice
to a highway thawed by salt
and when they took her home they said
"you're welcome"
and then they disappeared.

This is a rescue that is what it was.
It does not stand for something else.
I can't compare that rescue to anything—
though I know you will.

Caretaker

1

For years she'd only known his name was Morton,
a shadow Frank would talk to by the barn.
She'd seen his silhouette in four positions:
his back bent under the stalled mower's hood,
or prone on dirt beneath the pickup truck
or elbow jabbed backward on chainsaw rope—
always three strokes and then the low roar rose
to the house.
                    She knew his lanky lounge at rest,
leaning against the barn, the setting sun
behind, the dark straight stream of tobacco.

Most days he'd be out far beyond her sight
with bales and grain to feed his cows, or post-
hole diggers, rolled barbed wire, whatever he
would need on land they'd lent him in exchange
for work around their place. So they could stay.

2

On days he chored for them—he cut the grass
on the green and yellow Deere she used to drive
or mowed the banks that slanted to the creek,
always Frank's job—she could just make him out.
Though he was still a shadow from her window,
a long back curved above the wheel, a gray
sweatshirt, blue overalls, black baseball cap.

She finally saw his face, or what of it
she could, beneath the country cowboy hat
when he came up to till her garden plot.

In March she'd brought the supper in to Frank
and asked the question that she knew would take
another thing away:

Could Morton help
to till and tend her garden once Spring came?
It seemed an age before he said, "Of course—"
and then the old half-smile she'd missed for months—
"How else can summer mean your succotash?"

3

The first time they asked Morton in the house
it was so he could move their bed downstairs.
He went back up to help Frank down, then spoke
as she was tucking in the sheet: "Coyotes,"
was all he said as if Frank had asked him
a question.

4

Then he started coming more,
for lifting things, unsticking things that stuck,
but often he just took a porch-chair seat
and chewed tobacco, spitting out brown arcs
over the railing. "How's he doin' now?"
he'd ask when he heard her come out the door.
"'Bout the same," she'd say to Morton's back.

She still saw him around the barn as shadow,
or pulling weeds, black-hatted. But when face
to face, each time she thought he looked unlike
the time before. He'd hardly talk or glance
at her, but Morton bent an ear to where
Frank lay.

5

In June she picked a rose each day,
a Mister Lincoln she and Frank had ordered.
The catalog had called it "heaven's scent"
and so it filled his room, she thought. But now
there hardly was a space to put a vase.

Outside among the roses she had heard
the sounds from up the ridge. She knew, though she
had never heard such mournful calls as these.
"We've got coyotes," she told Frank, "I heard them."
He made to sniff the rose awhile, then whispered
"Remember Morton told us? Long ago?"

6

One day in August, just in from the garden
with corn to puree with some butter beans,
she heard a muffled cry from down the hall
and dropped the basket at the kitchen door.
Frank's voice was rasping out a cry for help:
Help me, Morton!
                                        She heard him as she ran.
And there was the caretaker, bending over,
as if Frank's chest and mouth were engines,
as if his hands could start up what had stopped.
But Morton shook his head and passed her by.

7

Into the night, into long afternoons
she made a wail that coyotes answered.
But in the Winter, nothing answered silence.
In Spring the quiet rabbits splurged on weeds.

8

She didn't realize until much later
when Morton left that room, he'd gone for good.
Then she recalled his pale eyes meeting hers,
that once, as he walked out. But she was wrought
and might have been mistaken. Anyway,
that time was long ago, back on the farm.
If she saw Morton now, she wouldn't know him.

Stealing Grace

Suspicion was always sneaking—
from mountain thicket to woodpile
from an offshore boat to the beach—
so I entertained one for decades.

Suspicion was whispered
in services beyond my belief,
signaled in signs I was blind to.
Worse, shouted so loud I lowered my ears,
printed so boldly and badly I shuttered my eyes.

But suspicion still sneaked.
Something called grace was being delivered to people not me.
For one thing you had to believe in the sense of the word itself
and there was no way in the world it made sense to me
except that I couldn't dance.
Couldn't move in the arms of a man to a musical beat.
Couldn't smack ball against racket before it had passed.
Bumped into doors, wrote words from the left, in short
was gauche.

I decided to steal it.
And that's why you've caught me here
lurking in library stacks under *G*,
studying grace and how to grab it.
Excuse me, excuse me,
I was just leaving—

emptyhanded but hopeful,
off to the mountains where there have been moments,
there have been times in absolute solitude
when, for no discernible reason
my body has stepped out and danced.

Blessing the Watersnakes

Unaware is the word that Coleridge used
and I'd try to explain to my sophomores
what I couldn't explain to myself.
But, yes, I see now, how it is
after the long sail down, the Doldrums, the deaths,
the hallucinatory orange sun. "Alone,
Alone, all, all alone."
Who could believe in anything?
Who could believe in anything?
But the Mariner saw the watersnakes
and blessed their beauty unaware.

An hour's drive up from sea level
there's a rise and a bend in the highway
where the Blue Ridge comes into view
like an ocean of gentle waves when
you're swimming among them, pushing
up with one foot against the squishy sand
to ride up over and down the swell
and I catch myself pushing the accelerator,
smiling unaware.

Today planting seeds, zinnia and cosmos,
the flakes off last winter's dead flowers
that can disappear from your hand if you don't
get them under the breeze and a few crumbs of earth,
my back was to the pathside wall of trumpet vine, raspberry,
honeysuckle, woven into the woof of locust trunks backed
by mountain's slope. When I turned

first I shivered, then I smiled. And then I smiled
at myself, eye level with a coppery snake.
Alone and smiling unaware.

Something gives way then, something heavy snaps
apart at my neck and slides weightily down my body.
and what have I done, not believing in anything,
to deserve this light air?